Jordan and Earl

by Bud Hamilton
illustrated by Arvis Stewart

Practice Decodable 88

Mc Graw Hill Education

Bothell, WA • Chicago, IL • Columbus, OH • New York, NY

MHEonline.com

Send all inquiries to:
McGraw-Hill Education
8787 Orion Place
Columbus, OH 43240

ISBN: 978-0-02-145444-0
MHID: 0-02-145444-2

Printed in China.

8 9 10 11 12 DSS 27 26 25 24 23

"Hurry up, Jordan!" called Earl. "You walk too slowly."

Jordan heard Earl, but Jordan was reading an Earth Day poster.

Jordan did walk slowly, and he stopped often. Jordan liked to search for things. He also liked to learn things as he walked.

Earl had to wait for Jordan a lot. Earl looked in a sports store window. He thought about a birthday gift for Jordan.

Jordan thought about his birthday, too. He looked at the sports equipment. He saw soccer balls. Perhaps he would get one.

"Hurry, Jordan. It will be dark before long," blurted Earl.
"It is still early. And we are not far," replied Jordan.

Jordan and Earl were going home. The boys had chores to do. Earl had to start dinner for the family soon.

Now Jordan thought about ice cream in the store. Did the clerks serve more peanut butter or peppermint ice cream?

"Hurry up, Jordan," urged Earl. Earl stopped at the corner to wait. Then Earl lifted his purple shirt and searched his pockets.

A patch of earth was next to the curb. Jordan looked down. He saw a gold shimmer in the dirt.

It was a key. Jordan picked it up and turned it over in his hands. It was Earl's key to the house!

Jordan looked over at Earl. He knew what Earl was searching for. Earl must have dropped the key.

Jordan marched over to Earl. "It is a good thing I am not in a hurry," he said.

"Why?" asked Earl.

Jordan held out his arm and showed Earl the key. Earl smiled. "It was a good thing this time," said Earl.

Jordan gave Earl the key. Then he started to run. "Hurry up," teased Jordan. "It will be dark before long."